SWAP YOUR TRIALS & CURSES FOR

AMAZING BLESSINGS

MM KIRSCHBAUM

SWAP YOUR TRIALS & CURSES FOR AMAZING BLESSINGS

By
MM Kirschbaum

I dedicate this publication to: JEHOVAH-MACCADDESHCEM. YOU ARE THE LORD WHO SANCTIFIES. LET YOUR NAME BE GLORIFIED ABOVE ALL THINGS
IN JESUS NAME – AMEN.

ISBN-978-1-937318-10-9
Copyright © 2013 by MM Kirschbaum
Swap Your Trials & Curses for Amazing
Blessings
Revised and Expanded Edition 2013
P. O. Box 1035
Anoka, MN 55303
prayerwelive@live.com
prayerwelive@aol.com

I appreciate and acknowledge modified names,
places and instances, respect privacy and
confidentiality. All Scripture quotations derived
from the Holy Bible, King James Version, and
Microsoft Windows Application 8 clip Arts and
Angel Clip arts from Dover Publication.

CONTENTS

CHAPTER ONE
UNWARRANTED CURSES

Curses are burdens, plagues, troubles, misfortunes, spells or magic. They are not new in the existence of humanity. They are multilayered hassles entrenched in the culture of life and the sources of many trials for a majority of us. Therefore, it cannot be covered randomly under a single title. While others may scoff at the mention of it, the outcome can be very unpleasant. In many cases, it must be fought fire-for-fire. Nevertheless, the purpose of this publication is to empower you as you read stories of life's trudging through. Why not go for the best crown if you have come thus far in life. This is not the time to be discouraged or quit. While others may scoff at the mention of it, the outcome can be very unpleasant. In many cases, it must be fought fire-for-fire.

As you read through this publication, I will appeal to you to 'change' your language. If you are swapping trails and curses for surprising blessings, it must also manifest in your words, in your mind and expressions.

I had to learn the lesson as well. As a convert to Christianity, it was one of the great disclosures from the Holy Spirit.

Before then, when something unpleasant was on the horizon, I would say, "That is how it should be." It was when I began to search the scriptures and made inquiries from the Holy Spirit that I understood these things.

I was foolishly running a race on the treadmill and counting the miles. Yes, I have covered some distance, but I have not moved from the same spot.

The reference is symbolic because of the words of Galatians 5:16-17 which states:

"This I say then, Walk in the Spirit, land ye shall not fulfil the lust of the flesh. For other flesh lusteth against the Spirit, and the Spirit against the flesh: and these are contrary the one to the other: so that ye cannot do the things that ye would."

After watching his house struck by lightning and his two horses' sudden disappearance, Alex was very worried. Just down the road near his house was a troublesome neighbor and land owner. They had series of arguments in the past over very minor issues but this time he was threating.

His complaint was regarding Alex's two old horses. He said, they were grazing on his land. Alex apologized but the man continued to threaten. He wanted Alex to pay for the grazing and the two horses taken away from his vicinity else, they would disappear. Not planning any confrontation, Alex walked away and kept his horses within his own compound.

A certain day Alex attended a town's meeting and saw his neighbor there. Quickly, there was a confrontation as the man continued to accuse Alex of letting his horses graze on his fields. Apologies and excuses did not help as the man looked through the window and called on the winds of fire. He commanded lighting to strike the horses and the house of the owner.

Alex ignored him and walked away. First, he did not believe in curses and did not expect such a wretched man with no family to affect his substance.

On reaching the house he checked the horses and they were not on his property. He drove out his car again in search of them. There was a slight drizzle then lightening. As he made the turn off his property, a bolt of light came from the sky and struck the loaded haystack. Turning back, he took out the fire extinguisher but the fire was fast and quick. He was overwhelmed. His other neighbor was half a mile away. He called the fire emergency and watched as his house burnt to the ground.

"But God is the judge: he putteth down one, and setteth up another. For in the hand of the LORD there is a cup, and the wine is red; it is full of mixture; and he poureth out of the same: but the dregs thereof, all the wicked of the earth shall wring them out, and drink them. But I will declare for ever; I will sing praises to the God of Jacob." (Psalm 75: 7-13)

Beloved, there are many churches with different types of menu. The recipe for these palatable looking sermons or dishes is not helping many people to grow and be strong.

As a result, I want us to reassess these two common assertions from our pulpits. This is critical because it is not helping many believers. Unplanned and unprepared, we are told to either ignore Satan or become fixated on his guiles. Hence, when our Lord Jesus is knocking on the door of our hearts we cannot hear Him.

"For I beheld, and there was no man; even among them, and there was no counsellor, that, when I asked of them, could answer a word. Behold, they are all vanity; their works are nothing: their molten images are wind and confusion. Isaiah 41:28-29.

" Thus saith God the LORD, he that created the heavens, and stretched them out; he that spread forth the earth, and that which cometh out of it; he that giveth breath unto the people upon it, and spirit to them that walk therein: I the LORD have called thee in righteousness, and will hold thine hand, and will keep thee, and give thee for a covenant of the people, for a light of the Gentiles; To open the blind eyes, to bring out the prisoners from the prison, and

them that sit in darkness out of the prison house.
I am the LORD: that is my name: and my glory will I not give to another, neither my praise to graven images. Behold, the former things are come to pass, and new things do I declare: before they spring forth I tell you of them."
Isaiah 42:5 to 9.

Can you see that we are giving God's glory to another unknowingly?
Many of us are carrying burdens initiated when we were not even conceived. One of the traps of the Satan is to convince you that your sins and burden is too much and so complex that God will not help you. Thus, you have come to the cross our Lord Jesus Christ and you refuse to abandon your burden at the foot of that cross. When you took a look at God on the cross, you became discouraged. You forgot that He rose on the third day and conquer death. He suffered that we may be heal.

"I have declared, and have saved, and I have shewed, when there was no strange god among you: therefore ye are my witnesses, saith the LORD, that I am God. Yea, before the day was I am he; and there is none that can deliver out

of my hand: I will work, and who shall let it?"
Isaiah 43: 12-13.

A woman carried her farm products from the
farm to a bus-stop. She was going to the market
to sell the items. The bus driver attempted to
assist her in placing the load in the baggage area
but this woman refused.
She said, "No, I cannot let you carry it into the
trunk. I have suffered and worked twice to get
this products. I prefer to carry it on my laps."
The bus driver informed her that the journey
was hours away and there was no need to
burden herself with such cumbersome load.
Moreover, seventy percent of the passengers
were going to her destination and have their
produce in the large trunk.
The woman replied that it could be that they
never worked as hard as she did on her farm. If
they had gone through what she went through,
they would all carry their loads on their heads.
When the driver realized the woman was
undeterred, he left her alone and proceeded on
the journey. Everything was quiet until three
hours later. This woman shouted that she has
no feelings on both her legs and feet.
The driver said, he could not stop abruptly in
the highway for such a case – it was against
company security policy.

Then the woman began to plead with everyone in the bus to help her with her luggage but no one volunteered.

She said, "Help me. You people going to the market understand the difficulties involved in getting the yield."

They replied her that, "Yes, we know. We worked just as hard as yourself if not harder. We cannot place our crops in the trunk of the bus and carry your own. Sorry madam - carry your luggage for yourself."

You see what is happening here? They blamed her for not placing her load in the trunk.

That is how many of us will be blamed for not placing their trials and curses before the cross of our Lord Jesus Christ. If we must swap our trials and curses for blessings, we must understand that we are dealing with a compassionate God.

We are not just anybody but believers in our Lord Jesus who has declared that He is the way and the truth. Remember, that all the hassles and suffering Jesus went through is for our sake. God is longsuffering and has endured our foolishness enough.

However, let us examine how He identifies Himself to us: "I am the LORD, your Holy

One, the creator of Israel, your King. Thus saith the LORD, which maketh a way in the sea, and a path in the mighty waters; Which bringeth forth the chariot and horse, the army and the power; they shall lie down together, they shall not rise: they are extinct, they are quenched as tow.

Remember ye not the former things, neither consider the things of old.

Behold, I will do a new thing; now it shall spring forth; shall ye not know it? I will even make a way in the wilderness, and rivers in the desert.

The beast of the field shall honor me, the dragons and the owls: because I give waters in the wilderness, and rivers in the desert, to give drink to my people, my chosen.

Isaiah 43: 15 to 20.

CHAPTER TWO
TRAILS THAT LEAD TO BLESSINGS

During a time when I was in deep meditation, fasting and vigil, a vision was revealed to me. I have narrated the vision in another publication titled, "FOR UNCOMMON BLESSINGS BE STRONG AND GOOD COURAGE." I will repeat it here just in case you have not read it.

This was how the vision went. I was in a church service. There was so much singing and dancing going on with interjections of prayers and amen. Everything appear as you will expect in a well-motivated church service led by a jolly well-dressed preacher. First, I observed some of the congregation members had white gowns on with matching caps. Secondly, some of the members had no clothes on – they were naked. This group did not appear aware that they were naked. In fact, they worshipped with the group that had flamboyant, colorful and regalia clothing in symphony – man and woman. In confusion and bewilderment, I took a closer look at the choir members and discovered they also had the same predicament as the church members. Yet, they continue to gyrate to the music from the church band. I moved over to an elderly gentleman who appeared knowledgeable and wearing a church regalia with shimmering edges. I tugged at the gown. It dissolved similar to the softness of butterfly wings. This happened with every tug on the gown. I watched in astonishment as each thread of these well-adorned and multi-colored gowns began to disintegrate.

It continued until the individual became naked. There was no sign of awareness or mindfulness. Now, I knew something was erroneous.

The Lord was showing me a vision entrenched in a mysterious and profound knowledge.

Glancing to the side of the pulpit wall, there was a fire-blazing sign which read: "THOSE THINGS WHICH ARE REVEALED BELONG UNTO THE CHILDREN OF GOD. BE STRONG AND OF GOOD COURAGE FOR THE VISION REFERS TO THE END TIME. BE STRONG AND OF GOOD COURAGE. BE STRONG AND OF GOOD COURAGE. BE STRONG AND OF GOOD COURAGE."

I prayed: "Open thou mine eyes, that I may behold wondrous things out of thy law. I am a stranger in the earth: hide not thy commandments from me. Make me to understand the way of thy precepts: so shall I talk of thy wondrous works. My soul melteth for heaviness: strengthen thou me according unto thy word. (Verses 27 to 28)

Give me understanding, and I shall keep thy law; yea, I shall observe it with my whole heart. Turn away mine eyes from beholding vanity; and quicken thou me in thy way. Hold me according unto thy word, that I may live: and let me not be ashamed of my hope. Hold thou me up, and I shall be safe: and I will have respect unto thy statutes continually. (Verses 116 to 117)

Then, the Holy Spirit began to enlighten me. This was the meaning of the vision which revealed in a form of explanation.

From the very beginning God created the heavens and the earth. Here at the same time. The earth, which is our dwelling was still unformed so God created the light. This He did by separating the light from the darkness. Again, we have a double or two-sided creation: the light and the darkness. From this point, He made the first day which turned out to be day and night. The Lord made sky, divided the waters below from the waters above the sky or heavens.

In another publication, I will deal with the cadre of heavens as explained to me by the Holy Spirit. For now it suffices that we move into the second day.

Then God made the waters under the havens to be fused together thus the dry land appeared. Which was called earth while the waters became the seas. So, earth and water was made at the same time. Another double-sided creation. We can go on and on up to the seven days of creation and the two sons of Adam and

Eve, Cain and Abel. Where am I going with these two-sided or double–sided analysis? It is to show you that blessings need the searcher to be strong and of good courage.

God made earth and heaven, then He made Adam out of dust, planted a garden in Eden, with the tree of life. This is the tree of knowledge of good and evil. The Garden of Eden was very beautiful to behold. But there was a command that every tree of the garden was available to Adam except the knowledge of good and evil. From this tree, he was not to have anything to do with it or he would definitely die. Now, God in His infinite kindness said, "It is not good for the man to be alone; I will make a companion for him." Though other companions such as animals existed during this period God wanted more for him.

God wanted him to have the best, to have a helper, an assistant. So, God made Adam to fall into a deep sleep and He made a woman from a rib taken from his body.

The first deceit was in the form of a question posted to Eve through the evil one. In a very simple and well-phrased sentence: "Has God really said, 'You shall not eat from any tree of the garden'?" instead of a yes or no answer, Evil received an answer with some explanation qualifying the no or yes.

It went like this: "We may eat of the fruit of all the trees of the garden except the fruit of the tree which is in the middle of the garden, for God has said, 'you shall not eat from it, nor shall you touch it; for if you do, you shall die."

Remember, she was not informed of this information directly by God but was passed on to her by Adam who received the directives from God.

But something happened that is critical to the whole scenario. Going further, the Bible made a comment that Eve saw that tree was good, she took its fruit and ate it.

Which means, if she was not attracted to the fruit, a million-sermon from the Evil-One would have entered one ear and come out from the other. This is similar to a class you do not like with a teacher who is a smooth talker. Since you hate the class from the beginning you will do everything to avoid it.

And if you somehow find yourself in that class, your mind will be somewhere else. Not even a joke from the teacher or instructor would be worth the student's listening time. The student would consider the class boring.

Well, we know that she gave Adam and the eyes of both of them were opened.

This is a spiritual connotation for it does not lead to blindness. They did or would not require assistance in getting around or attending to their physical needs. It only signifies that their eyes where opened but they could behold the glory of God.

Everything created or that comes into being has a side and the other side. To receive uncommon blessings you need to be strong and to be of good courage.

CHAPTER THREE
BALAK'S DONKEY

The Bible has an unusual verse in Numbers 5:23, "And the priest shall write these curses in a book, and he shall blot them out with the bitter water:" This should place our mind at rest that this illness has a prescribed medication.

That God is still in control of occurrences. The worst news to hear after any diagnosis is to be told there is no medication for it.

We would not care if the only available therapy came from some form of experimentation or the research. Nonetheless, this is not the situation because the issue of trails, curses or misfortunes are embedded in our DNA. It is a recognized phenomenon that is written out with necessary prerequisites.

The Bible recognizes and calls the matter to the open.

In Numbers 22:6 we observe this fascinating verse. "Come now therefore, I pray thee, curse me this people; for they are too mighty for me: peradventure I shall prevail, that we may smite them, and that I may drive them out of the land: for I wot that he whom thou blessest is blessed, and he whom thou cursest is cursed." This is a classic example of the perplexity of curses.

As the children of Israel continued on their journey, Balak the son of Zippor, king of Moab saw all that Israel had done to the Amorites. And Moab was sore afraid and distressed at the sight of the children of Israel. And Moab said unto the elders of Midian, "Now shall this multitude lick up all that is round about us, as the ox licketh up the grass of the field?" therefore, he sent messengers unto Balaam the son of Beor, to Pethor, saying, "Behold, there is a people come out from Egypt: behold, they cover the face of the earth, and they abide over against me: come now therefore, I pray thee, curse me this people; for they are too mighty for me: peradventure I shall prevail, that we may smite them, and that I may drive them out of the land: for I know that he whom thou blesses is blessed, and he whom thou curses is cursed."

And the elders of Moab and Midian departed with the rewards of divination for Balaam. He said unto them, "Lodge here this night, and I will bring you word again, as the Lord shall speak unto me."

And God came unto Balaam, and said, "What men are these with thee?"

And Balaam said unto God, "Balak the son of Zippor, king of Moab, hath sent unto me, saying, Behold, the people that is come out of Egypt, it covered the face of the earth: now, come curse me them; peradventure I shall be able to fight against them, and shall drive them out."

And God said unto Balaam, "Thou shalt not go with them; thou shalt not curse the people: for they are blessed."

And Balaam rose up in the morning, and said unto the princes of Balak, "Get you into your land: for the Lord refused to give me leave to go with you."

And the princes of Moab rose up, and they went unto Balak, and said, "Balaam refused to come with us." And Balak sent yet again princes, more, and more honorable than they. And they came to Balaam, and said to him, "Thus saith Balak, the son of Zippor, Let nothing, I pray thee, hinder thee from coming unto me: for I will promote thee unto very great honor, and whatsoever thou sayest unto me I will do: come therefore, I pray thee, curse me this people."

And Balaam answered and said unto the servants of Balak, "If Balak would give me his house full of silver and gold, I cannot go beyond the word of the Lord my God, to do less or more. Now therefore, I pray you, tarry ye also here this night that I may know what the Lord will speak unto me more."

And God came unto Balaam at night, and said unto him, "If the men be come to call thee, rise up, go with them; but only the word which I speak unto thee, that shalt thou do."

And Balaam rose up in the morning, and saddled his ass, and went with the princes of Moab. And God's anger was kindled because he went: and the angel of the Lord placed himself in the way for an adversary against him. Now he was riding upon his ass, and his two servants were with him. And the ass saw the angel of the Lord standing in the way, with his sword drawn in his hand: and the ass turned aside out of the way, and went into the field: and Balaam smote the ass, to turn her into the way.

Then the angel of the Lord stood in a hollow way between the vineyards, a fence being on this side, and a fence on that side. And the ass saw the angel of the Lord, and she thrust herself unto the wall, and crushed Balaam's foot against the wall: and he smote her again. And the angel of the Lord went further, and stood in a narrow place, where was no way to turn either to the right hand or to the left. And the ass saw the angel of the Lord, and she lay down under Balaam: and Balaam's anger was kindled, and he smote the ass with his staff.

And the Lord opened the mouth of the ass, and she said unto Balaam, "What I have done unto thee, that thou hast smitten me these three times?"

And Balaam said unto the ass, "Because thou hast mocked me: I would there were a sword in mine hand, for now I had killed thee."

And the ass said unto Balaam, "Am not I thine ass, upon which thou hast ridden all thy lifelong unto this day? Was I ever wont to do so unto thee?"

And he said, "Nay." Then the Lord opened the eyes of Balaam, and he saw the angel of the Lord standing in the way, with his sword drawn in his hand: and he bowed his head, and fell on his face. And the angel of the Lord said unto him, "Wherefore hast thou smitten thine ass these three times? Behold, I am come forth for an adversary, because thy way is perverse before me: and the ass saw me, and turned aside before me these three times: unless she had turned aside from me, surely now I had even slain thee, and saved her alive."

And Balaam said unto the angel of the Lord," I have sinned; for I knew not that thou stoodest in the way against me: now therefore, if it displease thee, I will get me back again."

And the angel of the Lord said unto Balaam, "Go with the men: but only the word that I shall speak unto thee that thou shalt speak."

So Balaam went with the princes of Balak. And when Balak heard that Balaam was come, he went out to meet him unto the city of Moab, which is on the border of Arnon, which is in the utmost part of the border.

And Balak said unto Balaam, "Did I not earnestly send unto thee to call thee? Wherefore camest thou not unto me? Am I not able indeed to promote thee to honor?"

And Balaam said unto Balak, "Lo, I am come unto thee: have I now any power at all to speak anything? The word that God putteth in my mouth, that shall I speak."

This story goes to show us that placing a curse on another or requesting another to do it only result in misfortune. When a person is overwhelmed with misfortunes or in a continuous circle of struggles it is time to explore Jesus Christ. From this story, we see how God Himself was already defending the children of Israel against the issuance of any curse on the way to take king of Moab plus the leaders of the medianite may use bribe but God is always on the throne.

As Balaam proceeded to see the king and the gathered elder an angel came between them, and the angle waylaying Balaam's donkey possible to employ another to place a curse. When Balaam set out to do the bidding of Balak the king of Moab, he went to the mountains of the East. He was supposed to, "Curse Jacob, defy Israel." But he did not. Instead he said, "How shall I curse, whom God hath not cursed? And how shall I defy, whom the Lord hath not defied?

For from the top of the rocks I see him, and from the hills I behold him Lo, it is a people that dwell alone, and shall not be reckoned among the nations. Who can count the dust of Jacob, or number the fourth part of Israel? Let me die the death of the righteous, and let my last end be like his!"

Balak was furious for he said, "What hast thou done unto me? I took thee to curse mine enemies, and, behold, thou hast blessed them altogether."

And Balaam said, "Must I not take heed to speak that which the Lord putteth in my mouth?"

Balak to Balaam to many spots on the rock, on the mountaintop, on the plain and asked for curses to be places on the children of Israel. When Balaam opened his mouth, his utterances where allegories and parables for he said: "Rise up, Balak, and hear; Hearken unto me, thou son of Zippor: God is not a man, that he should lie; neither the son of man, that he should repent: Hath he said, and shall he not do it?

Or hath he spoken, and shall he not make it good? Behold, I have received commandment to bless: And he hath blessed, and I cannot reverse it. He hath not beheld iniquity in Jacob, Neither hath he seen perverseness in Israel:

The Lord his God is with him, and the shout
of a king is among them. God bingeth them
forth out of Egypt;

He hath as it were the strength of the wild-ox.
Surely there is no enchantment against Jacob,
Neither is there any divination against Israel:

Now shall it be said of Jacob and of Israel,
What hath God wrought! Behold, the people
riseth up as a lioness, And as a lion doth he lift
himself up: He shall not lie down until he eat of
the prey, And drink the blood of the slain."
In frustration, Balak said unto Balaam, "Neither
curse them at all, nor bless them at all." But
Balaam answered and said unto Balak, "Told
not I thee, saying, All that the Lord speaketh,
that I must do?"

This did not stop here. It went on and until,
Balak's anger was kindled against Balaam, and
he smote his hands together: and Balak said
unto Balaam, "I called thee to curse mine
enemies, and, behold, thou hast altogether
blessed them these three times."

CHAPTER FOUR
X-MARKS THE SPOT

A woman recently rented a store-front with loan from her in-laws. But she never had a week without her money disappearing. No one came into the store and no one went out yet she could not account for missing money kept in small packets. One day at the bank she was narrating the story to a cashier-teller who told her that the last owner of that store had similar complains several times before he abandoned the store. As this lady was making this statement a senior staff overheard it and said it happened to the last two store owners not just one. She was very distressed because her in-laws fund were invested in the store.

A friend gave her a short story I wrote analyzing how to change your burses into blessings. The only tough spot for her was that she decided to take a fast on a thanks giving day. She had a peculiar vision of something being placed into the floor of the store. In fact she was able to X-marks the spot.

Awake, she told her husband who assisted her to some digging. And on the same spot as she saw it in the vision, she found a single key. With the key, she began to look around for what it could open when the husband noticed a hallow space as he walked around the place.

Underneath the floorboards they found a small compartment. Using the key, it fit perfectly. They opened it to find some small gold nuggets and old pictures. From then on, nothing happened again. She is still in the store and thriving.

In this other story I will title: "THEY CALL ME, MR. KEN" is from one of my publications: "REJUVENATE YOUR STAR." Just like it is possible to negatively affect one's destiny you so it is possible to affect ones star. We all have stars – that will be full explained in another context. Just before we leave this aspect, remember that the three wise men came looking for our Lord Jesus by following His star. Herod and his men also know the importance of the star and the ability to connect it with one's destiny.

If you suspect you are under a curse you will need to ask God to direct your steps. This is also means, 'moving to the other side' which means into the supernatural. It is here you can 'see' the whole story either in dreams, visions or instant manifestations. An example of in manifestations of the power can be found in the Second Book of Kings Chapter 6 from verse eight:

"Then the king of Syria warred against Israel, and took counsel with his servants, saying, in such and such a place shall be my camp. And the man of God sent unto the king of Israel, saying, Beware that thou pass not such a place; for thither the Syrians are come down. And the king of Israel sent to the place which the man of God told him and warned him of, and saved himself there, not once nor twice. Therefore the heart of the king of Syria was sore troubled for this thing; and he called his servants, and said unto them, Will ye not show me which of us is for the king of Israel? And one of his servants said, none, my lord, and O king: but Elisha, the prophet that is in Israel, telleth the king of Israel the words that thou speakest in thy bedchamber. And he said, Go and spy where he is, that I may send and fetch him. And it was told him, saying,

Behold, he is in Dothan. Therefore sent he thither horses, and chariots, and a great host: and they came by night, and compassed the city about. And when the servant of the man of God was risen early, and gone forth, behold, a host compassed the city both with horses and chariots.

And his servant said unto him, alas, my master! "How shall we do?" And he answered, "Fear not: for they that be with us are more than they that be with them."
Please observe this portion because of the next step of the prophet. He prayed.
"And Elisha prayed, and said, LORD, I pray thee, open his eyes, that he may see. And the LORD opened the eyes of the young man; and he saw: and, behold, the mountain was full of horses and chariots of fire round about Elisha.

And when they came down to him, Elisha prayed unto the LORD, and said, Smite this people, I pray thee, with blindness. And he smote them with blindness according to the word of Elisha.

And Elisha said unto them, this is not the way, neither is this the city: follow me, and I will bring you to the man whom ye seek. But he led them to Samaria. And it came to pass, when they were come into Samaria, that Elisha said, LORD, open the eyes of these men that they may see.

And the LORD opened their eyes, and they saw; and, behold, they were in the midst of Samaria. And the king of Israel said unto Elisha, when he saw them, my father, shall I smite them? Shall I smite them? And he answered, Thou shalt not smite them: wouldest thou smite those whom thou hast taken captive with thy sword and with thy bow? Set bread and water before them that they may eat and drink, and go to their master.
And he prepared great provision for them: and when they had eaten and drunk, he sent them away, and they went to their master. So the bands of Syria came no more into the land of Israel.

He prayed and the eyes were open. Many of us make decision with our physical eyes open but our inner eyes are closed- shut-down. We make life and death decisions, get married, get a job but our eyes are actually closed. Yes they are. Therefore, it is my prayer that in the mighty name of our Lord Jesus Christ, the Spirit of God will open your eyes and you will 'see,' amen.

Let us examine this passage from the book of Ezekiel chapter one. Prophet Ezekiel gave us a glimpse into the uncanny supernatural realm.

"Now it came to pass…as I was among the captives by the river of Chebar, that the heavens were unfastened, and I saw visions of God. And I looked, and, behold, a whirlwind came out of the north, a great cloud, and a fire unfolding itself, and brightness was about it, and out of the midst thereof as the color of amber, out of the midst of the fire. Also out of the midst thereof came the likeness of four living creatures. And this was their appearance; they had the likeness of a man. And every one had four faces, and everyone had four wings. And their feet were straight feet; and the sole of their feet was like the sole of a calf's foot: and they sparkled like the color of burnished brass. And they had the hands of a man under their wings on their four sides; and they four had their faces and their wings. Their wings were joined one to another; they turned not when they went; they went every one straight forward. As for the likeness of their faces, they four had the face of a man, and the face of a lion, on the right side: and they four had the face of an ox on the left side; they four also had the face of an eagle. Thus were their faces: and their wings were stretched upward; two wings of every one were joined one to another, and two covered their bodies.

And they went every one straight forward: whither the spirit was to go, they went; and they turned not when they went. As for the likeness of the living creatures, their appearance was like burning coals of fire, and like the appearance of lamps: it went up and down among the living creatures; and the fire was bright, and out of the fire went forth lightning. And the living creatures ran and returned as the appearance of a flash of lightning. Now as I beheld the living creatures, behold one wheel upon the earth by the living creatures, with his four faces. The appearance of the wheels and their work was like unto the color of a beryl: and they four had one likeness: and their appearance and their work was as it were a wheel in the middle of a wheel. When they went, they went upon their four sides: and they turned not when they went. As for their rings, they were so high that they were dreadful; and their rings were full of eyes round about them four. And when the living creatures went, the wheels went by them: and when the living creatures were lifted up from the earth, the wheels were lifted up.

Whithersoever the spirit was to go, they went, thither was their spirit to go; and the wheels were lifted up over against them: for the spirit of the living creature was in the wheels. When those went, these went; and when those stood, these stood; and when those were lifted up from the earth, the wheels were lifted up over against them: for the spirit of the living creature was in the wheels."

He observed that, "whithersoever the spirit wanted to go, they went..."
Subsequently, the spirit remains the driving and directing force. The wheels only went where the spirit guided it to go.

Why? Because, the spirit of the living creature was in the wheels. "When those went, these went; and when those stood, these stood; and when those were lifted up from the earth, the wheels were lifted up over against them: for the spirit of the living creature was in the wheels."

The spirit is the key. It is the spirit that makes it work. It is the functionality that is operating the essence of life. This is important for us to grasp.

CHAPTER FIVE
A GOOD PREPARATION

One day, I received an email from a friend
thanking God for the successful completion of
the brother's military mission abroad.

This person further stated that they can now
heave a sigh of relief that the brother was back
in the country.

That night, I had a very curious dream.

I saw that the brother of the caller was among a
group of soldiers on a mission but did not

return. I sent this person an email informing him of my dream. He replied back that it was impossible because they were on their way already. I apologized and went about my usual routine. But, I was shocked that it took days for the authorities to inform the family members. This maybe a result of bureaucratic snail-speed or other security matters. It was catastrophic. While, my friend and other family members thought they had completed their mission, they were all dead.

From this point on I am going to break down for you a series of practical prayers that you can use. We are following the directives of God by teaching your hands to war and your fingers to do battle. I believe and have no doubt in my mind that Christians who discard the Old Testament, for one reason or another are actually throwing the 'baby-and-bathwater' out. They are denying themselves a unique source of power. How can you have electrical cooker in the house and you are cutting the woods of the forest so you can just cook a meal?
Again, there are no contradictions but fresh revelations every time. Take advantage of your digital/electronic books and let us get to work swapping those curses and trials for amazing blessings.

The two-sides to a coin is the supernatural on one side and the physical component on the other. Yet, Jesus is the author and finisher of our faith who died, rose and said, "All authority belongs to me." He is the same yesterday, today and forever. He is the Unchangeable Changer (Hebrews 1:12.) He is the son of God, the Omnipresence, Omnipotence, "I AM." God is still on the throne. According to Psalm 8 from verse 4 - "What is man, that thou art mindful of him? And the son of man, that thou visits him? For thou hast made him a little lower than the angels, and hast crowned him with glory and honor. Thou made him to have dominion over the works of thy hands; thou hast put all things under his feet."

You will decide the number of days that will be convenient for you to complete the prayers. They will be in blocs of three, five or seven (3, 5 or 7.) You may repeat it, modify the wordings that suits you or replace a prayer point that does not affect your current situation.

There are seven separate segments for you. This will give you the opportunity to choose what prayer points best suits your needs. The most important key in this whole exercise is to place your trust in the Lord.

Do not look to the east or to the west, to north or to the south, to the right or to the left. I am positive that you will see the goodness of God in this land of the lying.

I cannot boast further for the Lord said: "But let him that gloried glory in this, that he understandeth and knoweth me, that I am the LORD which exercise loving-kindness, judgment, and righteousness, in the earth: for in these things I delight, saith the LORD," Jeremiah 9:24.

As usual, I pray and join with you in spirit according to Mathew chapter 18, verse18, that states: "Verily I say unto you, whatsoever ye shall bind on earth shall be bound in heaven: and whatsoever ye shall loose on earth shall be loosed in heaven." Therefore, we are going to do some binding and we are thank you because we know that it is already done in the name of Jesus - amen.

I call upon the gracious name of Lord Jesus and say directly to Him: "My Jesus, You said in verses 19 to 20, that, "Again I say unto you, That if two of you shall agree on earth as touching anything that they shall ask, it shall be done for them of my Father which is in heaven. For where two or three are gathered together in my name, there am I in the midst of them.

Father, give us the grace to be able to forgive those who have wronged us according to, verse 22 of the same chapter. We give God glory and pray this day that He will open our eyes and understanding in our endeavors in the name of Jesus, Amen."

Remember that nothing is too difficult for God to do for He is the Father, who wishes His children well. In Isaiah 43:19: He said, "Behold, I will do a new thing; now it shall spring forth; shall ye not know it? I will even make a way in the wilderness, and rivers in the desert." Believe that He will do a new thing in your life today. Have no fear.

Faith is the key that opens the door of possibilities and the measure of our faith is subjective. Therefore, be Strong and believing for prayer changes things and it is your route to amazing power.

1. Plan, organize and take any opportunity of privacy
2. Monitor your dreams and keep a notepad/pen nearby. The very first night is important. Do not stop or make any quick conclusions with your dreams except you have a special divine gift of

dreams and you are confident that what you see is what you get. I have my reasons because the dreams or visions may also manifest in bits or in parables which will be fully revealed as you conclude the prayers.

3. Spiritual matters are subtle but effective. It is good to have some patience and take it gradually.

4. You will have to observe some form of fast either by missing a meal or performing consecutive night vigils from 12 midnight to 3AM. During this period you will be praying, meditating and speaking good things into your life, Remember that: "We wrestle not against flesh and blood, but against principalities, against powers, against the rulers of the darkness of this world, against spiritual wickedness in high places" (Ephesians 6:12).

5. You will have three bottles of medium size drinkable water or a gallon size or equivalent. If you are using collected from a tap, use a moderate container that you can lift easily. Please, consider factors such as prescribed medications, age, physical, drowsiness, etc.

6. You will be praying into the water. This will be appropriately referred to as, 'your water." You will place it close to your mouth and speak to it. In this type of case and according to the Elishan Prophets, it will be repeated 21 times.

7. Find some private area within your abode where you will not be disturbing the other members of the family. I must confess that in dire times, I have found the bathroom or the kitchen as convenient praying grounds. When push comes to shove and you are desperate, you will clean these areas before the nightfall. Wipe the floor off with rags if there is any pool of water in any area. Keep the place fit to sit and if possible to stand or even kneel. Place a chair and a small stool and take into consideration your circumstances such as, wearing sturdy shoes and having your prayer items in one place, etc.

CHAPTER SIX
PRAYER SEGMENTS

There is nothing God cannot do. Please be certain about that fact. God is ALMIGHTY, ALL-KNOWING and His mercy endures forever. This is what you will need:

Segment One

It is necessary to give thanks to God for everything. Now, ask for forgiveness from God. Therefore, pray this point and modify accordingly.

"God, my Father I have done..........I know this is displeasing to you. Forgive me for the sake of your son, Jesus Christ. If you judge me or your children, who shall stand before your holy throne? Forgive me and my family in Jesus name. You are the beginning and the end, the Alpha and Omega. Be glorified; hear me, as I begin this prayer session in Jesus Name.

Have mercy upon me, O God, According to Your loving-kindness; According to the multitude of your tender mercies.

Blot out my transgressions.

Wash me thoroughly from my iniquity; cleanse me from my sin. For I acknowledge my transgressions, my sins are always before me. Against You, You only, have I sinned, forgive me. I was brought forth in iniquity, and in sin my mother conceived me therefore, purge me of hidden sins and I shall be clean. Wash me, and I shall be whiter than snow. Hide your face from my sins and blot out all my iniquities in the name of Jesus. (Psalm 51, NKJV)

Segment Two (Plead the blood of Jesus over yourself body, soul and spirit.) Speak these words:

"I plead the blood of Jesus over my body, spirit and soul. Have mercy upon me, O God, wash me thoroughly and I shall be clean. I know and believe that my intentions will be fulfilled. Here are my intentions ……….. (Mention your desires.) Create in me a clean heart and let me hear joy and gladness in my home. Renew a steadfast spirit within me and do not cast me away from your presence. Do not take Your Holy Spirit from me but restore to me the joy of your salvation. Uphold me by your generous Spirit in in the name of Jesus."

1. Give me the grace to forgive, and I ask for forgiveness concerning these matters………… (Mention your hurts.)
2. Do not despise me. My heart is broken, help me concerning………...and let me find favor with you concerning ………...in the name of Jesus.
3. There is nothing that you cannot do, my God. I will not afraid. Hear my cry about……. in the name of Jesus. Thou art my Lord. Restore peace to my heart concerning ………...in the name of Jesus.

3. Whatever wind of oppression, depression, arrangement, agreement that is a source of confusion in my life will be neutralized in the blood of Jesus. Therefore, I will not be afraid or discouraged in Jesus name!

Segment Three
"Deliver me from the guilt of bloodshed, O God, You are the God of my salvation, deliver me completely and let my tongue sing aloud of your righteousness in the name of Jesus. Lord, open my eyes that I may see in spirit and open my mind that I may understand my situation, in Jesus' name. My God, You do not desire sacrifice but a broken spirit hear me now, do not despise me; lift my burden off me now by for I am broken. I need You in my life the name of Jesus."
"Lord, I will not be afraid, but I will stand still, and see Your goodness in this land of the living.

"My God, my Father I have done this………..
(Mention what you feel guilty about). I know this is displeasing to you. Forgive me for the sake of your son, Jesus Christ. If you judge me who shall stand before your holy throne? You are the beginning and the end, the Alpha and Omega. Be glorified; hear me, as I begin this

prayer session in Jesus Name. Have mercy upon me, O God, According to Your loving-kindness;

According to the multitude of your tender mercies by the name of Jesus. Blot out my transgressions. Wash me thoroughly from my iniquity; cleanse me from my sin by the name of Jesus.

My God, let me not be put to shame. I am requesting that........... blessing of life, of hope, of love be mine today in the name of Jesus.

Segment Four

This is how you will handle this segment. Take a glass of water or bottle (just one) and repeat this prayers twenty-one (21 times) Use faith you will be adding the water to your bath.

Pray:

1. Today, I am casting away all hatred, detestation, disgust, dislike, and loathing, animosity related to me through any curse or curses or misfortunes. Just as Pharaoh's chariots and his army where cast into the sea of nothingness, I do herby cast everything into the sea in the name of Jesus.

2. According to the Book of Deuteronomy 28:45 I have harken to the Lord therefore none of these curses shall come upon me. I shall pursue and overtake those who try to destroy me because I have harkened unto the voice of the LORD my God.

3. No person, nothing, no spirit of any form, in any way, with whatever name or whosoever, whatever will henceforth bring hatred into my life. If any of this is interfering in my affairs in any way, it shall FAIL in the name of Jesus. They shall fall down as the horse and its rider. Therefore, I take control of my life for my name is blessed. I am blessed in Jesus name – amen.

4. According to Isaiah 54:17 - No weapon that is formed against me shall prosper; and every tongue [that] shall rise against me in judgment I shall condemn. This [is] the heritage of the servants of the LORD, and their righteousness [is] from the LORD who is my Father.

Segment Five

1. According to Deuteronomy 30:19, heaven and earth was to recorded this day and set before me life and death, blessing and cursing: therefore I have chosen life that both I and my family may live.
2. I shall find ease and the sole of thy foot shall have rest in the name of Jesus.
3. My heart shall not tremble nor my eyes fail nor their sorrow in my mind in the name of Jesus.
4. I am not a candidate for curses. Therefore any curse placed upon me in any way is rejected in totality. Just as I reject any seed of poverty in my life, so do I reject every shaky foundation, in my life in the name of Jesus?
5. My Father, My God, You are the God of my salvation; deliver me. Holy Spirit, relieve my heavy heart for who is blameless in your holy presence, my God?
6. Hear my cry and restores peace to my heart in the name of Jesus.
7. Surely goodness and mercy shall follow me all the days of my life; and I will dwell in the house of the Lord forever - amen

Segment Six

Please, pray chapter 23 of the Book of Psalms. I will suggest you repeat this exactly 21 times. What I the purpose of this? Use the pray in the water above and repeat this prayer 21 times. The purpose of this psalm is to contain fear and embolden your heart. This will enable you may be able to make better and sensible decisions. You may do that now and we can continue.

You can also encourage the heart of your family members or friends by giving them this secret. You do not have to shop for it. Just water and speak the word – and you have power in it. According to the prophets of old, the power in your tongue is greater than the power in the mouth of another. So, go ahead: SPEAK LIFE INTO YOUR LIFE NOW.

"The Lord is my shepherd; I ...... (You name) shall not want. He make me to lie down in green pastures: he leaded me beside the still waters. He restored my soul: he leaded me in the paths of righteousness for his name's sake. Yea, though I ......(you name) walk through the valley of the shadow of death, I ......(you name) will fear no evil: for thou art with me; thy rod and thy staff they comfort me. Thou prepares a table before me in the presence of mine enemies: thou anoints my head with oil;

my cup rennet over. Surely goodness and mercy shall follow me all the days of my life: and I ...... (you name) will dwell in the house of the Lord forever in the name of Jesus."

(Now, add some to your bath. Prepare for your dreams – monitor them – this is important.)

Segment Seven
Please pray this three times. Fill in the spaces as you go along with your name – calling it out loud.

"I .....(Mention your name) abide in the Shadow of the Almighty, I dwell in the secret place of the Most High, I abide under the shadow of the Almighty.
 Therefore, I .....(Mention your name) will say of the LORD, He is my refuge and my fortress: My God; in him will I trust.   Surely he shall deliver me from the snare of the fowler, And from the noisome pestilence. He shall cover me with his feathers, and under his wings shalt I trust: his truth shall be my shield and buckler. I will not be afraid for the terror by night; Nor for the arrow that flieth by day; nor for the pestilence that walketh in darkness;
Nor for the destruction that wasteth at noonday. A thousand shall fall at my side,

And ten thousand at my right hand;
But it shall not come near me. Only with my
eyes shalt I behold and see the reward of the
wicked. Because I have made the LORD, which
is my refuge, Even the Most High, my
habitation; there shall no evil befall me,
Neither shall any plague come near my
dwelling. My God shall give His angels charge
over me, to keep thee in all my ways. They shall
bear me up in their hands, lest I dash my foot
against a stone.

I …..(Mention your name) shall tread upon the
lion and adder:

The young lion and the dragon shalt I trample
under feet.

My God has promised hat as I continue to love
Him, He will deliver me:

He will set me on high, because I have known
his name. When I call upon him, He will answer
me.

He will be with me in trouble; He will deliver
me, and honor me. With long life will He
satisfy me and show me His salvation in Jesus
name - amen.

CHAPTER SEVEN
REJUVENATE YOUR STAR

In conclusion: This is for you in case you have
not read: "REJUVENANTE YOUR STAR'
one of my past publications. Here it goes:
That first night, our man Ken sat alone before
the Lord in the spare bedroom.
He has about six days to reject the offer, return
to his post. His wife, Sara, was not interested in
such a proposition and the children became

bargaining commodities. Ken wept inconsolably for, the very thing that he feared is about to overtake him. They have sold their house back in the city because he was one hundred percent self-assured that nothing could go wrong. After doing the prayers above 23 times, he drank some of the water and, used a part with his bath. That night, he had a dream. This is how Ken narrated it:

"I saw many bright stars, blazing, shining and glittering. The stars began to dance around; it was such a beautiful sight. It was amazing. I watched in amazement as these twinkling stars moved further away from where I was standing but continued to dazzle. Others simply glittered and stayed on the same spot. I noticed a man in black clothes walking with audacity around.

He came over to a star and covered it with a piece of cloth and the shine dulled immediately. He walked past others and went over to another and tried to pull it down but it will not budge. He fell down many time and was bruised himself in his attempt he tried about five but nothing happening until he went to the sixth when he discovered how easy it is. With one yank, he pulled the star down. Right in my presence, this star was gone. I just knew it was not good. I was afraid. Then I began to recite the Lord's praise used during my spiritual bath:

MY GOD, YOU ARE THE MOST HIGH GOD, THE MOST HIGH GOD, THE MOST HIGH GOD. MY GOD, YOU ARE THE MOST HIGH GOD, THE MOST HIGH GOD, THE MOST HIGH GOD
Then, I began to speak to my star. I said, my star, you are God given to me. You have shown for me brightly and I am happy. Therefore, whatever is clouding it or whosesoever is clouding it expose this person in the name of our Lord Jesus.
Several names came to mind, even my sinister, mother, my uncle and an old relative but I just kept saying, "Lord show me the person, open my eyes that I may see.
I saw this person checking out covered stars. As he came to a star I knew it was mine. I just knew it. He lifted the lid off the star for a moment and covered it back. Then he walked away to another star. At this point, I was petrified with fear. I have never had such spiritual experience all my life. For the very first time, I believed that there is indeed, 'another side.' I remember when our Lord said, "Let us go to the other side."

Ken continued with same prayer session plus 12 hours of fasting.

Ken informed me that on the third night, he laid on the floor, weak from fasting when the dream he had on the first day repeated itself but there're was a difference. This time, the man took out the lid and the star dazzled brightly that he saw the face of the person in a glimpse. It was the pastor of their new church! It was the pastor that literally took his wife's attention from the family. Suddenly, there was a knock on the door. He was awake.

Sara, his wife came into the spare bedroom door with an interesting story.

She was having an affair with the pastor who was much older, richer and really, really knew had to talk himself into the heart of anyone. When their affair began, Ken's wife was worried that Ken might find out about it. But the worldly pastor told her to bring her husband's personal life details, hair, comb/brush and his toothbrush.

This was an easy assignment for her. Though she was aware the pastor maybe dubious, she under-estimated his diabolic plans.

Somehow, she became very guilt-ridden and the spirit of God judged her and troubled her that she could not sleep, eat or rest.

She want's forgiveness, restoration, will be will to return back to their former station. They are both young and many opportunities abound if they remain as a family.

Continue to speak to your star. It is your God given star. You know what to do now, you know how to do it. Speak to your star. It is your God given star, your star is your leading light. It is well with you in the name of Jesus –amen.

About the Author
MM Kirschbaum (MMK) RN-BC, CMSRN,
(Med-Surg) BSN, LLB, BA is well-travelled,
speaks/writes/understands several languages,
graduated BSN-Cum Laude (NAU),
President's, DEAN's list. A prolific writer with
over 100 eBooks with several currently in print.
An instinctive evangelist with prophetic
understanding of enigmatic and mystifying
spiritual matters. Member of Prayer-We-Live
and Elishan Intercessors bounded by faith in
the supernatural powers of God.

Other Publications by Same Author
Bringing Down Showers of Blessings
The Compelling Power of the Holy Spirit
Moving Beyond Your Fears and Worries
Triumph Over Marital & Relationship Worries
A TIME TO PROSPER
DEEP SECRETS THAT CAN SAVE YOUR
MARRIAGE & RELATIONSHIP
Command your Blessings of the Day and of the
Night
Prevailing Over Witchcraft and How Marriages
Are Plagued
Prevailing Over Witchcraft

GET YOURSELF FREE FROM EVIL
COVENANT

COMMAND YOUR BLESSINGS OF THE
NIGHT

COMMAND YOUR BLESSINGS OF THE
DAY

ANGELS WILL LIFT YOU UP

HOW TO SPIRITUALLY MAKE HIM TO
LOVE YOU AGAIN!

DREAM HEAVENLY DREAM THAT
PROSPERS YOU

PROSPERITY: A FRESH BEGINNING

DELIVER ME FROM MY FRIENDS FOR I
KNOW MY ENEMIES

WHEN GOD SAYS YES WHO CAN SAY

HAS GOD ABANDONED ME?

OVERCOMING YOUR GOLIATH

THOSE THAT SOW IN TEARS WILL
REAP IN JOY

FEAR NOT FOR I AM WITH THEE

I RISE ABOVE IT ALL

I WILL NOT LET YOU GO UNLESS YOU
BLESS ME

SWAP YOUR TRIALS & CURSES FOR
AMAZING BLESSINGS

WE HATE EACH OTHER BUT WE SLEEP
WITH EACH OTHER

OPEN MY MINE EYES, THAT I MAY
BEHOLD WONDROUS THINGS

Listening to the STILL SMALL VOICE
FROM YOUR MOUTH COMES POWER
GOD IS STILL ON THE THRONE
I SHALL NOT DIE BUT LIVE
LET NOT MY ENEMIES TRIUMPH OVER
AT THE EDGE OF BREAKTHROUGH
FRESH IN THE SCHOOL OF ADVERSITY
FAVOR IS MY NAME
OUR FRANTIC SEARCH FOR HOPE
LET THE WINDOWS IN HEAVEN OPEN
FOR ME
YOU CAN STAND-OUT IN THE CROWD
INFLUENCE OTHERS TO LIKE YOU
My Refuge and My Strength
A very present help in trouble
LORD, DELIVER ME FROM THOSE WHO
HATE ME
MY HUSBAND IS CHEATING & I KNOW
THE PERSON
In thee, O LORD, do I put my trust; let...
LORD, do I put my trust; let me never...
TAKING CONTROL OF YOUR
MARRIAGE
GET YOURSELF FREE FROM EVIL
COVENANT
REJUVENATE YOUR FADING STAR
OVERCOMING ENEMIES IN YOUR
MARITAL HOUSE...
WHY DOES MY HUSBAND HATE ME?

LORD, DIRECT MY STEPS TO PROSPER
DEALING WITH THE FEAR OF FEAR
Book One
ATTRACT: AT FIRST SIGHT
GET HIM BACK NOW - 7-DAYS VERSION
HOW TO RETRIVE YOUR STOLEN
BLESSINGS
MY LOVE IS UNFAITHFUL
NEVERTHELESS I WAN...
HOW CAN I ATTRACT LOVE IN JUST
THREE DAY.
GET HIM BACK NOW 3 DAYS
GET HIM BACK NOW 5 DAYS VERSION
GET YOUR NO-BAGAGGE
LOVE/RELATIONSHIP
I WILL PROSPER ME AGAIN
A Step into the Supernatural
U are FRUSTRATED? EXPLORE
POSSIBILITIES...
GOD WHO DOES GREAT THINGS
Why Do I Keep Worrying? Part two
LORD! Hear my Cry
Lord Hear my cry
Simple (really simple) prayer-rites to A...
SELF HELP (5 Days Version) Rebuild your
Lord, Hear my Cry
PROSPER-MY GOD CAN AND WILL
FOR YOUR UNCOMMON BLESSINGS
ONLY BE STRO...

2013 PREDICTIONS PROPHECIES OCCURRENCES...

Why do I keep worrying? Part One

2013 PREDICTIONS PROPHECIES & LORD! HEAR MY CRY Part One

An Appeal to the GOD of the Living 7-sim...

Self Help: Rebuild your MARRIAGE secretly...

Why do I keep worrying? {Part Three}

Simple (really simple) prayer-rites to A...

Obtaining Supernatural Favor

DESPITE THE SITUATION I WILL PROSPER

OVERCOME FEAR IN UNCERTAIN TIMES

2013 Your Power in Stressful Times

Rebuild Your Marriage Secretly/Supernatural...

"I Offered my Soul for Fame"

AS THEY HARVESTED, DRONES OF LOCUST FELL...

If Only you just Look Up

RESTORE YOUR MARRIAGE AGAIN

YOU HAVE THE POWER

ATTRACT LOVE - a simple prayer

Self Help: The Sudden Caregiver

Angelic Visions

Rebuild Your Marriage Secretly/Supernatural...

www.ingramcontent.com/pod-product-compliance
Lightning Source LLC
Chambersburg PA
CBHW060536030426
42337CB00021B/4294